Native Americans

Comanche Indians

Caryn Yacowitz

Heinemann Library
Chicago, Illinois

Customer Service 888-454-2279

Visit our website at www.heinemannlibrary.com

Photo research by Alan Gottlieb
Printed and bound in the United States by Lake Book Manufacturing, Inc

07 06 05 04 03
10 9 8 7 6 5 4 3 2 1

Library of Congress Cataloging-in-Publication Data
Yacowitz, Caryn.
Comanche Indians / Caryn Yacowitz.
v. cm. -- (Native Americans)
Includes bibliographical references and index.
Contents: The Southern Great Plains -- The Comanche come to the Plains -- Horses and Comanche riders -- Hunting buffalo -- Tipis and travois -- Comanche clothing -- Families and bands -- Brave warriors -- Games and contests -- The Great Spirit -- Settlers arrive -- Broken promises -- The Comanche today -- Learning Comanche.
ISBN 1-40340-302-3 (lib. bdg.) -- ISBN 1-40340-509-3 (pbk.)
1. Comanche Indians--Juvenile literature. [1. Comanche Indians. 2. Indians of North America.] I. Title. II. Native Americans (Heinemann Library (Firm))
E99.C85 Y33 2002
978.004'9745--dc21

2002006322

Acknowledgments
The author and publisher are grateful to the following for permission to reproduce copyright material: pp. 4, 5 Raymond Bial, Urbana, IL.; p. 7 Art Resource; p. 8 North Wind Picture Archives; pp. 9, 11, 13, 18, 23, 24 National Museum of American Art, Washington, D.C./Art Resource; p. 10 National Museum of the American Indian, Smithsonian Institution, Neg.#02/1364; pp. 12, 14, 27L Western History Collections, University of Oklahoma Libraries; p. 15 National Anthropological Archives, Smithsonian Institution, Neg.#1775A; p. 17 National Archives, Neg.#165-A1-15; p. 19 The Thomas Gilcrease Institute of American History and Art, Tulsa, Oklahoma; p. 20 Comanche, Ledger Book, c. 1880-89, paper, pencil, ink, and watercolor, 17.5 x 25.4 cm, Gift of Richard A. Lent in honor of Mr. And Mrs. C. L. Lent, The Art Institute of Chicago; pp. 21, 28 Marilyn "Angel" Wynn/Nativestock; p. 22 Joslyn Art Museum; p. 25 Glenbow Museum Archives, Neg.#NA 1234-5; p. 26 Museum of the Great Plains; p. 27R National Archives 075-ID-93; p. 29 Michael Pope/Lawton Constitution; p. 30 courtesy Comanche Language Committee.

Cover photograph by Corbis.

Special thanks to LaDonna Harris for her help in the preparation of this book.

Some words are shown in bold, **like this.** You can find out what they mean by looking in the glossary.

Contents

The Southern Great Plains

The Southern Great Plains stretch across parts of the states of Oklahoma, Texas, Kansas, and New Mexico as well as parts of Mexico. Rolling grasslands seem to go on forever. There are very few trees. It is a land of wide open spaces and big, blue skies.

Summers here are very hot. Winters are very cold. Many feet of snow and ice cover the plains during winter storms. The wind blows across the plains all year long. Some people think the plains are just big and empty. Other people think this is a beautiful and special place.

The Comanches Come to the Plains

Long ago, the Comanches were probably part of the Shoshone people. They lived in the forests of the Rocky Mountains. This area is now the states of Wyoming and Montana. In the late 1600s, some of the Shoshone left the Rocky Mountains. They moved south to the Great Plains in order to hunt the buffalo. These people became the Comanches.

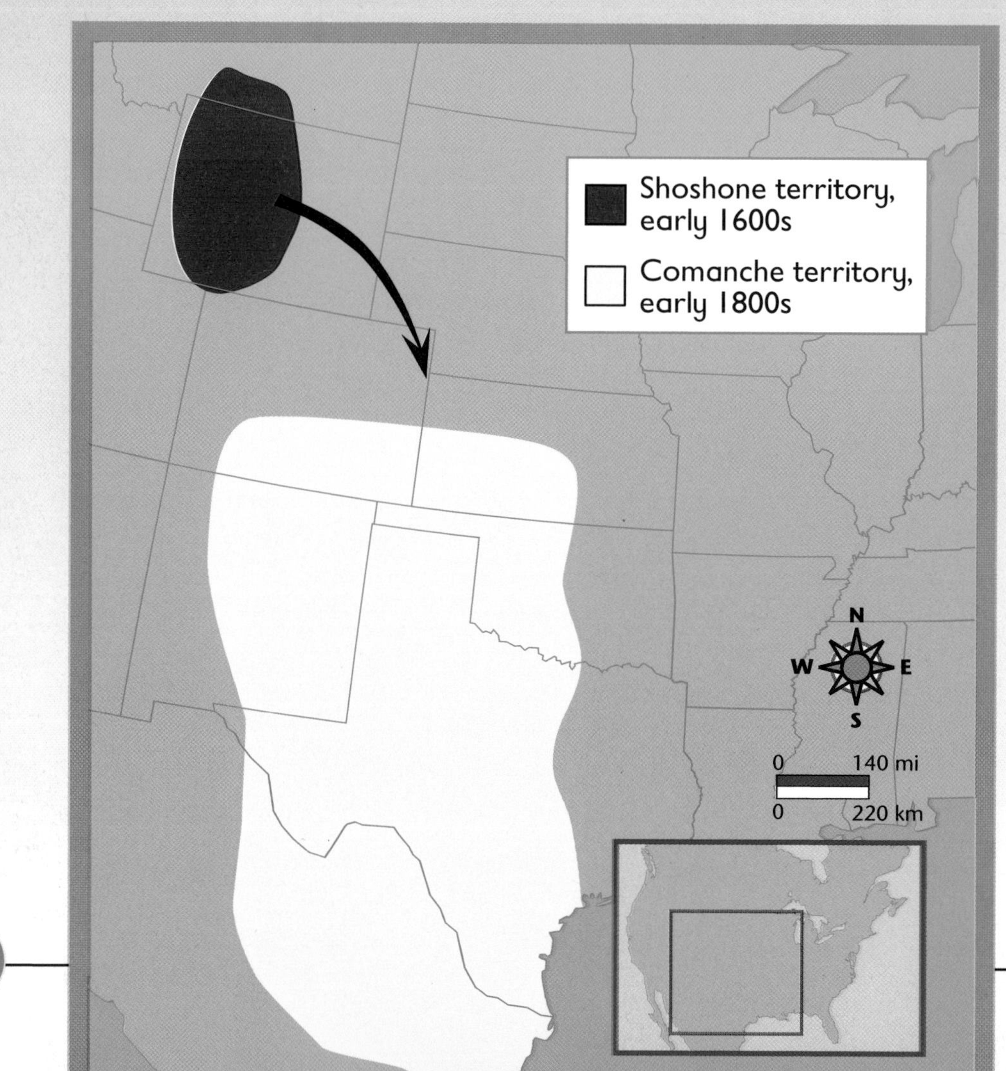

The Comanches called themselves *Nʉmʉ* or *Nʉmʉnʉh.* Both words mean "the people." They spoke a language that was like the Shoshone and Ute Indian language. Comanches were new to the Great Plains. Other **tribes** already lived there. The Kiowa tribe became friends and **allies** of the Comanches.

*This painting shows Comanche **warriors** ready for battle.*

Horses and Comanche Riders

When the Comanches first came to the Great Plains, they hunted buffalo on foot. This was very difficult and dangerous. In the early 1700s, they discovered an animal that would change their lives forever. It was the horse. There were no horses in North America until Spanish **settlers** brought them from Europe.

*A Comanche **warrior** could shoot a gun from under the neck of his **galloping** horse.*

Buffalo were not afraid of wolves. This George Catlin painting shows how Comanches sometimes hid under wolf skins to hunt.

The Comanches quickly became excellent horse riders. They learned to train horses better than any other **tribe.** Children learned to ride horses before they could walk. Comanches hunted buffalo and fought wars on horseback. Having horses made a Comanche powerful. Some Comanches had herds of over 1,000 horses.

Hiding Under Wolf Skin

George Catlin was an artist who traveled around the West. He made paintings of the Indians and how they lived. Look carefully at the painting above. One of the people hiding under a wolf skin is drawing. It is George Catlin. He put himself in the painting.

Hunting Buffalo

Over 60 million buffalo once roamed the Great Plains. The Comanche people followed the buffalo herds. They used bows and arrows or long **spears** to strike the buffalo in the heart. Everything the Comanches needed came from the buffalo—food, clothing, houses, tools, toys, and more. They had over 300 uses for the buffalo.

*The Comanches made **saddles** from buffalo bones.*

The Comanches never killed buffalo or any other animal for sport. They killed only what they needed to live.

The Comanches ate some parts of the buffalo raw. They ate these parts where the animal had been killed. They brought the buffalo back to camp, where the meat was **roasted** or boiled. They cut the rest into thin strips and dried them in the sun and wind. Once the meat was dried, it would not rot. The dried meat was like what some people call "jerky" today.

Inapʉ

Some of the dried meat was pounded together with buffalo fat and wild berries to make *inapʉ*. *Inapʉ* was high in energy. It was an important winter food for everyone in the **tribe. Warriors** ate *inapʉ* when they were away from camp. About 50 pounds (23 kilograms) of *inapʉ* could be made from the meat of one young buffalo.

Tipis and Travois

The Comanches lived in cone-shaped houses called *tipis* (TEE-pee). *Tipis* were warm in winter and cool in summer. It took twelve to fourteen buffalo **hides** to make a *tipi* cover. Women helped each other sew the hides together. Then they stretched the hides over long, straight poles made from pine or cedar trees. The women owned the *tipis.* They would put the *tipis* up and take them down.

It took less than half an hour to take down a tipi *and get it ready for travel.*

This painting shows a dog fight happening as the Comanches leave camp. Some of the dogs are pulling travois.

Before the Comanches had horses, they used dogs to move the *tipis.* They attached a *tipi* pole to either side of the dog or horse. The *tipi* cover was folded and placed across the poles. This kind of sled that Comanches used to pull things was called a travois (tra-VOY). The Comanches used the travois to move *tipis,* food, and other **belongings.**

Comanche Clothing

Men and older boys wore a **breechcloth,** which was a piece of soft **buckskin** that went between the legs. It was held by a belt at the waist. They also wore buckskin **leggings** and moccasins. Later, after Comanches met white **settlers,** the men wore long cloth or buckskin shirts.

This Comanche man, Burgess Looking Glass, is wearing traditional clothes.

These girls might be sisters. Their dresses are decorated with beads.

Comanche Dress

Comanche men, women, and children were proud of their appearance. They washed their hair with a natural shampoo made from the **yucca** plant. They painted the part in their hair red or yellow. Men often wore long braids that they decorated with fur, feathers, beads, or cloth.

Women and girls wore buckskin dresses with beads and other decorations. They wore moccasins. They used natural plant dyes to color their clothing. In winter, Comanche men, women, and children wrapped themselves in warm buffalo **hide robes.**

Families and Bands

Comanches lived in large groups called **bands.** The bands were made up of many families who lived and hunted together. Bands could be as large as 3,000 people. In every band, people were taught to have respect for their relatives. The bands were named for the foods they ate. Some of the bands were called Buffalo Eaters, Antelope People, Timber People, Wanderers, Honey Eaters, Root Eaters, and Liver Eaters.

*The Comanche bands did not get together for big **ceremonies** like other **tribes.***

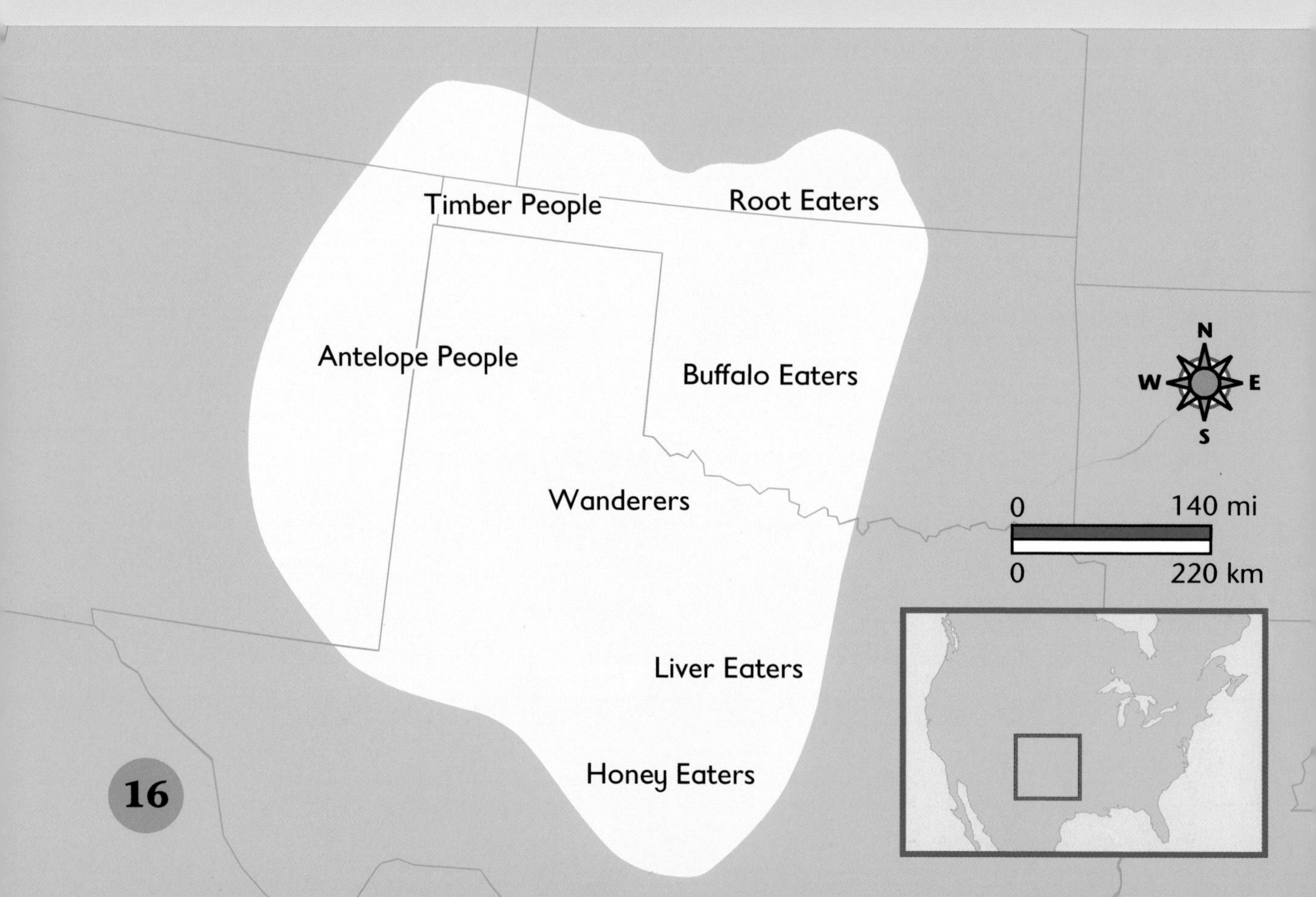

All the members of a Comanche family helped one another.

Each band had its own leaders. The most important qualities for a leader were **wisdom,** bravery, and **generosity.** Each band had a main leader. Each band also had a leader for peacetime and a leader for war. People often moved from one band to another. Different bands joined together when they had to fight an enemy.

Growing Up Comanche

Comanches believe children should be treated with kindness. Adults never hit or spanked children. Instead, they scolded or ignored a bad child until the child behaved better.

Brave Warriors

The Comanches were brave fighters. The most daring thing a **warrior** could do was touch his enemy in battle. This was called counting **coup.** Comanches believed it was much braver to touch an enemy than kill him. Any man could become a leader. If he was brave and people trusted him, they would follow him into battle. The Comanches fought to **protect** their land.

*This Comanche warrior is shown with his buffalo **hide** shield and weapons.*

Enemy Capture

Sometimes enemy women and children were captured during battle. They became part of the Comanche **tribe.**

Comanche warriors never left behind a wounded friend.

A warrior never **surrendered.** Rather, he would **stake out** by tying himself to a stake in the ground. This meant he was ready to die in battle. Comanche warriors would often risk their lives to rescue a staked-out warrior.

Comanche Medicine

Religion is an important part of Comanche life. Each person must understand his or her **medicine.** This is a person's special strength or talent. In the past, a young man would go out alone into nature. He would not eat for several days. He hoped to have a **medicine dream.** This dream would show him his strengths. Often, he saw an animal in the medicine dream. The animal became his **symbol** and **protector.**

This drawing shows a Comanche man's medicine dream. The wolves around the man gave him the power to find animals to hunt.

This Comanche man has strong medicine. He is sharing his musical talent at a ***ceremony.***

Today, each Comanche still seeks his or her own medicine. Everyone—including young children—has medicine. They must share it. People with strong medicine must be **generous.** Being a leader, playing music, creating art, cooking, singing, playing a sport, or knowing languages are all things that could be a person's medicine.

Games and Contests

The Comanches love games and contests of all kinds. Horse races, kick ball, arrow-shooting contests, and wrestling matches were enjoyed by Comanche men and boys. People also liked to bet on who would win the contests. Sometimes they would bet blankets or money.

*Horse racing was enjoyed by many Indian **tribes.** Riders also learned skills that helped them in battle.*

These men and boys are playing a Comanche game.

A guessing game popular with both men and women is called the hand game. Each team passes small bones or sticks from hand to hand while singing special songs. They try to confuse the other team. The object of the game is to guess who has the sticks or bones. Today, Comanches still love to play the hand game.

Settlers Arrive

From about 1720 to 1850, the Comanches ruled over the Southern Great Plains. During this time, they traded with some **tribes** and fought with others. Sometimes they fought with Spanish and French **settlers** who came into Comanche territory. The Comanches could **protect** their land because they were excellent riders and brave **warriors.**

This group of Comanche warriors is about to attack a group of settlers in a wagon train.

Buffalo bones piled up across North America. There were 60 million buffalo in the United States in 1800. By 1895, there were only 1,000.

But in 1845 Texas became part of the United States. Thousands of settlers began pouring into the Comanche homeland. Some settlers formed a group called the Texas Rangers. They wanted all the land for the new settlers. The Texas Rangers fought the Comanches for the land. The Comanches fought back, and many died. Other Comanches died from the **diseases** the settlers brought with them.

The Buffalo Are Killed

The United States government decided to kill all the buffalo. They knew that without the buffalo, the Comanches and other tribes would starve. Buffalo were killed all over the Great Plains. Their bodies were left to rot.

Broken Promises

In 1867, the United States government forced many Comanches into Fort Sill **Agency** in Oklahoma. The Comanches were forced to sign the **Medicine** Lodge **Treaty.** This treaty set up a Comanche **reservation.** But they could no longer move freely around the Great Plains. Instead, the government promised to give them food and homes as payment for the land it had taken.

Comanches often had to wait for food that the United States government had promised to give them.

Quanah Parker

Chief Ten Bears

Some Comanche **bands** were not at Medicine Lodge. They did not sign the treaty. These bands did not want to give up their way of life. Their leader, Quanah Parker, led them during a hard time. They had to give up their life of freedom on the Great Plains and learn to live on the reservation. Quanah Parker **surrendered** in 1875.

Chief Ten Bears

Ten Bears was another great Comanche leader. He did not want his people to be forced to live on the reservation. "I was born upon the **prairie** where the wind blew free and there was nothing to break the sun," he said. "I was born where everything drew a free breath. I want to die there and not within walls."

The Comanches Today

Today, there are about 10,000 Comanche people. Most live in Oklahoma. They are farmers, teachers, lawyers, nurses, and doctors. They encourage their children to go to college. The Comanches were always brave **warriors.** During World War II, Comanche code talkers helped the United States win the war. They used the Comanche language to send secret messages the enemy could not understand. Today, many Comanches join the United States Army, Navy, or Air Force.

Code talker Charles Chibitty has traveled around the United States telling people about his experiences in World War II.

Today, Comanche children participate in traditional ***ceremonies.***

Celebrations are a way for young and old to honor Comanche history and **culture.** The National Comanche Fair is held each September at Fort Sill Military Base. It is a time to visit relatives and old friends, dance, enjoy Comanche art, and eat traditional food. Every July, the big Homecoming **Powwow** takes place in Walters, Oklahoma.

Learning Comanche

Today, children study the Comanche language. A dictionary of the Comanche language is being written. This dictionary will include the hundreds of words that Comanches have for different kinds of horses. Learning the songs, dances, and language helps keep the Comanche **culture** alive and strong.

These twin girls are wearing shirts that have Comanche writing on them.

Glossary

agency government office in charge of projects in an area

ally (more than one are called allies) friend

band group of people

belonging something a person owns

breechcloth piece of clothing that covers the area from the waist to the knees

buckskin deerskin leather made soft by tanning

ceremony event that celebrates a special occasion

coup strike or blow

culture way of life of a group of people

disease sickness

gallop run very fast

generous willing to give or share; generosity is the quality of being generous

hide skin of a large, dead animal, usually with the fur still on it

legging covering for the leg

medicine for the Comanches, a person's special skill or talent

medicine dream dream in which a person understands his or her special skill or talent

powwow Indian gathering or celebration

prairie large flat area with a lot of grass and few trees

protect keep from harm or danger

religion system of spiritual beliefs and practices

reservation land kept by Indians when they signed treaties

roast cook over a fire

robe long, loose piece of clothing

saddle seat used to ride a horse

settler person who makes a home in a new place

spear long, straight weapon with a sharp blade at one end

stake out tie oneself to a piece of wood in the ground to show one is ready to die in battle

surrender give up

symbol something that stands for something else

treaty agreement between governments or groups of people

tribe group of people who share language, customs, beliefs, and often government

warrior person who fights in battles

wisdom good judgment that comes from the experience of life

yucca tall plant with long, stiff leaves

More Books to Read

Ansary, Mir Tanim. *Southwest Indians*. Chicago: Heinemann Library, 1999.

George, Charles. *The Comanche*. San Diego: Greenhaven Press, Incorporated, 2003.

Noble, David G. *101 Questions about the Ancient Indians of the Southwest.* Tuscon, Ariz.: Western National Parks Association, 1998.

Index